HAIKU AND HUMOUR

A COLLECTION OF INTERNATIONAL
POETRY EDITED BY

JILL DARRAGH

First published 2014.

Published by Rangitawa Publishing, Feilding, New Zealand.

Copyright Jill Darragh 2014.

All rights reserved,

No part of this book may be reproduced in any form or by any means without the prior consent of the publisher.

www.rangitawapublishing.com

rangitawa@xtra.co.nz

ISBN 978-0-473-27399-6

CONTENTS

HAIKU

Djurda Rozik (1st)	8
Michael Connell (2nd)	8
Marios Schismenos (3rd)	9
Anne Hollier Ruddy (4th)	9
Helen Buckingham	10
Carol Burrows	11
Michael Connell	14
Julian Ciupitu (H. Comm.)	17
Igor Damnjanovic (H. Comm.)	18
Tracy Davidson	19
Petya Gleridis	22
Jutta Heitland	24
Jenna Kanell	25
Ron C. Moss	26
Milena Mrkela	27
Fern Paulussen	28
Minh-Triet-Pham	30
Patricia Prime	33
Djurda Rozic	35
Anne Hollier Ruddy	36
Marios Schismenos	38
Dinos Crisis	39
Keith Simmonds	40
Sandra Simpson	41

Brandon Snap	42
Darren Stein	43
Carole A. Stewart	45
Kenneth Surridge	47
Eduard Tara	48
Dermano Vitasovic	50
Klavdija Zbicajnik	51
Jill Darragh	52

HUMOUR

Tracy Davidson (1st)	54
Carole A Stewart (2nd)	55
Jutta Heitland (3rd)	56
Carol Burrows	58
Carole A. Stewart	60
Jill Darragh	62

From the Editor

In 2013 Rangitawa Publishing held a poetry competition called Haiku and Humour. There was a wonderful response from poets all over the world. This is a collection of the best entries. It is quite astonishing how much can be achieved in three simple lines of blank verse. These selected haiku illustrate the wonderfully emotive and evocative moods this form of verse can achieve.

I would like to send my thanks to all who participated in the competition. To those who were not successful, please continue to work at your poetry. I have taken the liberty of adding some of my own poems to this book but obviously these were not judged!

As with all digitally published books we do our best to proof read and eliminate errors. If any reader finds a mistake please email us and we will correct the file.

Please enjoy reading this collection.
Jill Darragh January 2014.

The Illustrators

Marian Moseley A.N.E.A

Marian is resident in Cornwall, England. She started experimenting with ipad painting in 2012 when she was ninety two. She has continued to explore the medium and develop her style and will be ninety four in 2014.

Kylie Miri Thwaites

Kylie has a Fine Arts degree from Wanganui Polytechnic, New Zealand. She has exhibited in several Matariki exhibitions at Waitangi in the Bay of Islands and also in Whangarei.

Fritha May Johnston

Fritha is a pupil at Halcombe School, Manawatu, New Zealand. She will be nine years old in 2014.

These talented women are my family. Marian is my mother, Kylie, my daughter and Fritha my granddaughter.

HAIKU

DJURDA ROZIC   Croatia

all these shiny roofs

and just enough moonlight to

tuck in every tile.

1st prize

MICHAEL CONNELL   New Zealand

Home squats aloof, but

smirking, knowing my leaving

was only a whim.

2nd prize

MARIOS SCHISMENOS   Greece

at the first sunlight

seven happy roosters yell

a new day is here.

3rd prize

ANNE HOLLIER RUDDY New Zealand

Bright little lemons

Punctuate the tree outside

Like Christmas baubles.

4th prize

HELEN BUCKINGHAM

United Kingdom

taking the bus home
through fields ploughed yesterday
now furrowed with snow.

feared diagnosis
my therapist neighbour sighs
"Japanese knotweed"

red coats, yellow boots...
a four foot high fire dragon
blazes through the snow.

CAROL BURROWS

New Zealand

Slippery Snakes

coiled ready to spring

cobras head rises visible

above the terrain

sugar cane hides the

slippery sliding brown snake

snatching at his prey

soft silky smooth skin

camouflaged green black and brown

beware rattle snake

Domesticated Haiku

broken fingernail

annoyingly snags stockings

hung by the chimney

brilliant red polish

chips and cracks appear everywhere

on the rough sidewalk

child scribbles on walls

with multi-coloured crayon

portraits of passion

Fritha May Johnston – mixed media – 2013.

MICHAEL CONNELL

New Zealand

Road writing shows where
hidden services all lurk.
No surprises for the trades.

Cars prowl, cruising streets
in a disorderly way
searching for red lights.

Autumn always does
its annual palette thing
so nothing new there.

Fritha May Johnston - 2013

Shame the claret ash

doesn't come up with a drink.

Wouldn't it be grand?

On the bird bath rim,

blackbird hops, wings akimbo

before he plunges.

Marian Moseley – ipad painting – 2012.

JULIAN CIUPITI

Romania

early morning light —

how she deletes with lipstick

overnight kisses

(Highly commended)

new Sistine Chapel —

a rainbow puts on the sky

first touch of colour

extinguished fireplace —

imperceptibly her body

heats up the Sunday

IGOR DAMNJANOVIC

Serbia

one legged

in shallow water of canal

the white stork hunting

(Highly commended)

Translated by Durda Vukelie-Rozic.

TRACY DAVIDSON

United Kingdom

Wild forget-me-nots

How your memory struggles

To remember me

By the winter moon

I see the cold bare branches

Of your wasted limbs

With the first snowflake

The light fades from your blue eyes...

Peace after the storm

December sunrise

a brood of early ducklings

skating on thin ice

branches bare of leaves

stretch like skeletal fingers

reaching for the sky

Kylie Miri Thwaites – acrylic on wood.

deserted park bench

the memories of courtship

swallowed up by mist

PETYA GLERIDIS

Bulgaria

behind the mountains
the full moon – a playful fawn
chasing clouds' shadows

the silver pin
on the space cadet fleece cloak
the moon's nestled in

in tiny white cup
the dark espresso of night
the Milky Way winks

Marian Moseley – ipad painting – 2012

JUTTA HEITLAND

New Zealand

Depressing grey day
Daily life is what it is
Just stamina counts

Thoughts revolve around
Kid's laughter and memory
Break out and feel new

Insight shows the way
Move forward and don't return
Living luck of life!

JENNA KANELL

Cinnamon Lovers

Her skin, white and smooth:

Intoxicated kisses

beneath auburn curls.

She tastes like thyme

Stirred in hot water, for tea-

Chamomile for sleep.

Kylie Miri Thwaites – acrylic

RON C. MOSS

Tasmania

a dark amber glow
from dad's old tool shed window...
the scent of oiled wood

late call to dinner
mother opens the back door
to light our way home

tired young cowboys
stars fill their plastic tepee
through rips in the sky

MILENA MRKELA

Serbia

the birds on the wire

calmly follow the news

under their feet

Kylie Miri Thwaites – acrylic on wood.

FERN PAULUSSEN

New Zealand

Anxiety

Legs made of jelly

My heart surges in my throat

No, I can't, I'm scared

My fingers flail

Flittery, jittery hands

Stop, be still, don't move

My neck is a spring

My head bobbles, wobbles, jerks

Enough, I'm done. Run

Fritha May Johnston – Stencil 2013

MINH-TRIET PHAM

France

lush autumn forest -
a lonely fly agaric
brighter than the sun

Hollywood Sweet Gum –
unforgettable memory
of the best first kiss

summer holidays
the birds' and cicada's song
more melodious

ragged rusty bikes
remembering getaways
with my dear father

shooting stars shower
in the middle of pastures
a cozy camp fire

Black Metal concert
on the high voltage lines
old famished ravens

lost under moonlight
a little bit less alone
with my own shadow

cool winter's twilight

fear of burning my fingers

with a mulled wine glass

Marian Moseley – ipad painting 2012

metal zoo railings

in the breath of the white wolf

Alaska's hugeness

PATRICIA PRIME

New Zealand

early summer warmth
in the half-opened flower
a tiny dewdrop

a midsummer's day
no-one walking in the park
except for myself

solitary lunch
in the company of ducks
beside the river

DJURDA ROZIC

Croatia

night of hunter's moon

wings of owl cutting hush

and breath of its prey

life in a small town

he is a social climber

his dog is OK

Marian Moseley – ipad painting 2012

ANNE HOLLIER RUDDY

New Zealand

The camellia

Keeping beauty to itself

Droops all its red heads

A sparrow takes sips

From my old cup and saucer –

Our own communion

MARIOS SCHISMENOS

Greece

    the many changes

    characterizing its life

    pretty butterfly

    the golden soft sand

    and the clear blue seawater

    look great together

Kylie Miri Thwaites – acrylic.

DINOS CRISIS

Greece

<u>Always fight, always live</u>

When the night will come

Queen Crisis will rule and smile;

Most humans will cry.

When our life is black

evil demons seem happy.

Hope cannot stand it.

Fighting for justice

the angels are among us.

Warm Day arises!

KEITH SIMMONDS

United Kingdom

the echo of light

in the stillness of silence...

a lingering dawn

starry-eyed lovers

kissing under the full moon...

scent of lime blossoms

a flag of freedom

riddled with huge bullet holes

blowing in the wind

SANDRA SIMPSON

New Zealand

life as a stepchild –

mother's favourite flower

the red hot poker

vernal equinox

the thump-thump of a rabbit

under my tyres

chilly afternoon

sparrows work their way across

a sunflower patch

BRENDON SNAP

United States

Spring: a love begins.

Autumn: they grow apart now.

Winter: a swift death

Cancer ages you

Like Autumn's kiss on oak leaves.

Dry and crumbling.

Gray moss swaying in

tonight's gentle breeze like lost

spirits in a dance.

DARREN STEIN

Australia

An aspect of parenthood

Child's pet guinea pig

Bought for love and company

But I clean its mess

Cockroach

Roach in the kitchen

Perhaps it's time to call the

Exterminator

Fritha May Johnston 2013

<u>The Educator</u>

An English teacher

Trying hard to teach Haiku

A failure at both

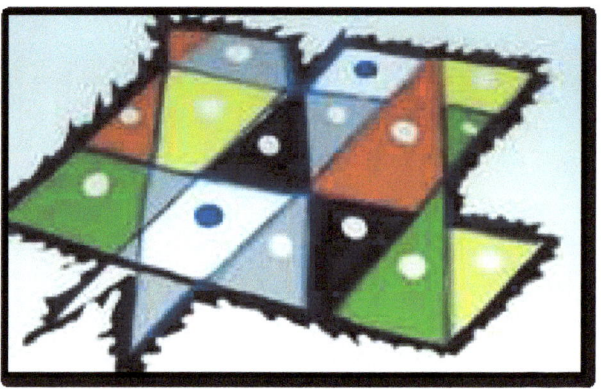

Marian Moseley – ipad painting 2012

CAROLE A. STEWART

New Zealand

Paua and kina
emptied shells on sunlit sand
Tangaroa's treasure.

With shooting star speed
one death swapped for another
squid rocket to beach.

Pohutukawa
blossoms red in summer heat
New Zealand Christmas

Hill tops pierce through

the thick white mist of morning;

magpies echo call

Upside down to sip

the bliss of harakeke

tui sway the stem

Kiwi on the tiles

terracotta embedded

hundreds on my roof

Marian Moseley – ipad painting 2012

KENNETH SURRIDGE

New Zealand

motorway puncture
recently separated
she breaks down again

sticky afternoon
girl in the shop window pings
her bikini strap

the youngest of three
polishing grandpa's medals
asks about Burma

EDUARD TARA

Romania

The flamingos step
to the edge of the darkness -
first light of dawn

Dive into the blue –
the red throated loon returns
covered in sunlight

The end of summer –
the call of the lone seagull
into the twilight

Kylie Miri Thwaites – acrylic

DERMANO VITASOVIC

Croatia

the autumnal days...
the ploughshares are furrowing
the rays of the sun

down the dusty road
imprinted droplets of rain
into thirsty dust

just before the beaks
and delivered to the tails
the heavenly blue

KLAVDIJA ZBICAJNIK

Slovenia

toothless cat waiting
at the door of his master
a famous dentist

hunter returning
small lying zebra scares him
when he cross the road

blue pants drying on
morning wind too close to the
coast of naked man

JILL DARRAGH

New Zealand

The pool crazed with ice
is puzzling for the gold fish.
Their sky is solid.

Water lilies float
on a deep, dark, calm lakeside.
Lotus position.

Passing the dead tree
the old woman barely looks.
Memory keeps it green.

Fritha May Johnston - 2013

HUMOUR

TRACY DAVIDSON

United Kingdom

Bottoms Up!
(A Royal Wedding Limerick)

We raised our glasses to the Royal pair

Oohed and aahed at Kate's dress and hair

But the most memorable thing

Amid the pomp and the bling

Was the shapeliness of Pip's derriere!

(1st prize)

CAROLE A. STEWART

New Zealand

Industrial Dispute

'Polyester, nylon, rayon,' she said

'create shocking static when worn in bed.

Electrified unsought nightmares begin,

causing wakeful hours of friction within.

Insomnia takes the spark from the night.

Even passions abate, faced with this plight.

Simplicity, nature's products I say

or nothing at all, for sleep or for play.'

(2nd prize)

Kylie Miri Thwaites – acrylic

JUTTA HEITLAND

New Zealand

When John and Joe to Wellington went

they saw two houses cheap to rent

one was too small

the other too tall

so they decided to stay in a tent.

The weather was a freezing affair

glacial cold raindrops ran down their hair,

they became mad

and then they got sad

what should they do in their despair?

They stumbled outside as fast as they could

and tripped over the peg as if they should.

The tent gave way

the boys in dismay

Wellington's wind cleaned up their goods.

Crestfallen and tired John and Joe

couldn't believe their misfortune and woe.

Looked at each other

bursting with laughter

drank Bordeaux with nowhere to go.

(3rd prize)

Marian Moseley – acrylic on slate

CAROL BURROWS

New Zealand

Consequences of a great life

life sometimes makes you sick

mother nature plays dirty tricks

now days I droop and sag

like a well-used vacuum bag

lines and hollows by the miles

a road map invades my dial

not so very nice to see

but behind it all I'm still me

my hair turned white overnight

it's quite a scary sight

blue eyes have faded fast

well hidden though behind the glass

sunken cheeks sunken lips

the fat has shifted to my hips

turkey neck what the heck

I'm just an aging wreck

a life well lived with plenty of fun

and too many hours spent in the sun

enjoy each moment love laugh be happy

who knows you could end up like me?

CAROLE A. STEWART

New Zealand

GOOD HUMOURED OR NOT

You say you have no sense of humour

But I have seen your eyes shine

And your mouth curve with pleasure

Heard your appreciative laugh

Your integrity refuses to

Pretend that things amuse when they do not:

Better the honest response

Than the crackling of indiscrimination.

MISS BARBIE QUEUE

I'm Miss Barbie Queue

and thrilled to meat you.

I'm the summer queen

of alfresco scenes.

When the climate's hot

I'm right on the spot

and my embers glow

with a little blow.

I give heat for steak

that tastes really great

when it is subdued

by my sultry mood.

My backburner's fire

Will feed your desire

I'm your Barbie Queue

and thrilled to meat you!

JILL DARRAGH

New Zealand

It's hard to write a haiku!

I wrote you a haiku

I thought you'd be impressed

But when I gave it to you

It did not pass your test.

You said

Just three lines you've written

To tell me that you're smitten!

You make me feel so worthless

You make me feel quite mirthless!

I explained

I muddled up my syllables

My words were far too long

My seasons were invisible

Your comments make me miserable!

You yelled

You *can* write a sonnet

An ode or villaneuve.

Put your back into it

Show me you've got verve!

I sighed

It's perfectly obvious I was mistaken in writing you a haiku

I was foolishly in error to think you'd be impressed.

When I arrived tonight and gave it to you

It was never going to pass your stringent test.

You don't like my brevity,

You don't like my levity,

You make me feel a failure.

In future

I'll just email yer!

The Poet's Muse

Joan Hunter Dunn is dead,

the obituary read.

She, a poet's love, is gone;

passed on.

When she walked the Surrey fields

in sensible shoes, laced and low heeled,

did she value his perfect rhymes

 and reminisce about the times

of green English lawns, tennis and tea?

Silky summer nights when he and she

danced late at country club balls,

Joan bare shouldered, wearing pearls?

And as she aged, this poet's muse,

she may have smiled, most amused

at idyllic scenes he composed.

Her youth and charms in such warm lines

redolent of better times.

Her life described upon the pages

enjoyed by many through the ages.

Unrequited though, the poet's love,

for her heart he never won.

There never was a Joan and John,

just Mr Betjeman and Miss Dunn.

Sadly, now they both are gone.

(With apologies to the late Sir John Betjeman)

Roaring Forties

The wind weasels up your trousers

And ferrets down your sleeves.

It creeps like moles

In very dark holes,

And rabbits at your knees.

It badgers your belongings,

And beavers at your bod.

It makes you feel quite ratty

Which isn't very odd!

Marian Moseley – ipad painting 2012

Rangitawa Publishing

Fiction

The Case of the Distant Relative

Creating Infinity

Milly Feather

The Rangitawa Collection 2013 (short stories)

Non-fiction

By Invitation

www.ingramcontent.com/pod-product-compliance
Lightning Source LLC
LaVergne TN
LVHW010026070426
835510LV00001B/3